Words Unbound

The Labyrinth of Derrida and Wittgenstein

The Curious Philosopher

Copyright Page

© 2023 by The Curious Philosopher

All rights reserved. No part of this book may be reproduced in any form or by any electronic or mechanical means, including information storage and retrieval systems, without permission in writing from the publisher, except by a reviewer who may quote brief passages in a review.

This book is a work of non-fiction. Unless otherwise noted, the author and the publisher make no explicit guarantees as to the accuracy of the information contained in this book and will not be held responsible for any errors or omissions.

Published by Omniterra Media Inc

First Edition

Visit the author's website at www.curiousphilosopher.com

Disclaimer

The views and opinions expressed in this book are those of the author(s) and do not necessarily reflect the official policy or position of any other agency, organization, employer, or company. The contents of this book are for informational and educational purposes only and are not intended to serve as professional advice, diagnosis, or treatment.

The information provided in this book is believed to be accurate and reliable as of the date of publication. However, it may include some errors or inaccuracies, and no warranty or guarantee is provided regarding the accuracy, timeliness, or applicability of the content.

Readers are encouraged to consult with professional philosophers, educators, or other qualified professionals where appropriate for personalized advice. The author(s) and publisher shall not be liable for any loss, damage, or harm caused or alleged to be caused, directly or indirectly, by the information or ideas contained, suggested, or referenced in this book.

By reading this book, the reader acknowledges and agrees that they are solely responsible for how they interpret and apply the information contained herein.

This book may also include references to other works, studies, and sources. These references are provided for further reading and exploration and do not imply endorsement or validation of the specific theories, viewpoints, or interpretations presented in those works.

Chapter 1: Introduction - The Convergence of Thought

Imagine two brilliant minds from different times and places, each with their own unique ideas about language and its mysteries. This is the story of Jacques Derrida, a French philosopher, and Ludwig Wittgenstein, an Austrian-British thinker. Though they never met, their ideas dance around similar themes but in different rhythms. Our journey begins with an introduction to these two intellectual giants and their contributions to the world of philosophy. But more than that, it's a journey into understanding how we use words and what they truly mean.

Jacques Derrida: The Enigmatic Explorer of Language

Jacques Derrida, born in Algeria in 1930, was a philosopher who loved to play with words. He believed that language was like a bottomless pit – the more you try to define something, the more meanings emerge, like a never-ending story. Derrida's main idea, called "deconstruction," is about peeling back the layers of meanings in texts, much like unraveling a tightly wound ball of yarn. He encouraged us to question everything we read and not to take words at face value. Derrida taught us that there's always more than meets the eye in the world of words.

Ludwig Wittgenstein: The Architect of Language Games

On the other hand, Ludwig Wittgenstein, born in Austria in 1889, was a thinker who saw language as a tool, much like a set of building blocks. He introduced the concept of "language games," which suggests that the meaning of words comes from how we use them, not just from their definitions in a dictionary. Wittgenstein believed that the way we speak and write is shaped by the rules of our 'games' – be it in science, art, or everyday chatter. He wanted us to see that understanding language is like understanding a game: once you know the rules, everything makes sense.

The Meeting of Minds: Derrida and Wittgenstein

This book is not just about Derrida's deconstruction and Wittgenstein's language games as standalone ideas. It's about exploring how these two philosophies intersect and where they diverge. Think of it as a conversation between two great thinkers, with us as the mediators, trying to find common ground and appreciating their differences.

As we delve deeper into their ideas, we'll explore the very fabric of language and meaning. How do we make sense of the world around us through words? How do our words shape our reality? These are some of the questions we'll ponder upon.

So, buckle up for a thought-provoking journey. Whether you're a seasoned philosopher or someone just curious about how language shapes our world, this exploration is designed to be engaging and accessible to all. Together, let's unravel the mysteries of language and meaning through the eyes of Derrida and Wittgenstein. Welcome to "Words Unbound: The Labyrinth of Derrida and Wittgenstein."

Chapter 2: The Architects of Language

Imagine language as a vast, intricate building, with countless rooms and corridors, each filled with different stories and secrets. In this chapter, we'll meet two master architects of language: Ludwig Wittgenstein and Jacques Derrida. Each of them approached the construction of language in their unique way, offering us fascinating insights into how we communicate and understand our world.

Ludwig Wittgenstein and His Language Games

Let's start with Wittgenstein. Picture a child learning to play a new board game. At first, the rules seem confusing, but as they play, they start to understand how each piece moves and how to win. Wittgenstein believed language works in a similar way. He said that words are like game pieces, and their meaning comes from the 'games' we play with them – these games being the different contexts in which we use language.

For example, think about the word 'bat'. In sports, it's something you hit a ball with. In nature, it's a flying mammal. The word is the same, but its meaning changes based on the 'game' we're playing – sports or zoology. Wittgenstein wanted us to understand that words don't have fixed meanings. Instead, their meanings are as varied and dynamic as the different 'games' we play with them.

Jacques Derrida and Deconstruction

Now, let's turn to Derrida and his idea of deconstruction. Imagine a novel. As you read, you understand the story based on the words on the page. But what about the ideas, the implications, the things that are hinted at but never fully said? Derrida believed that to truly understand a text, we need to look beyond what is written. He encouraged us to think about what's not being said, to question and 'deconstruct' the text, to uncover layers of meaning that aren't immediately obvious.

Derrida's deconstruction is like taking a magnifying glass to language. He asks us to look closely at words, to see how they interact with each other, and how they can mean different things in different contexts. It's like a puzzle where every piece (word) can change the whole picture (meaning).

Language: A Living, Breathing Entity

Both Wittgenstein and Derrida showed us that language is not a static set of rules or a fixed code to decipher. It's a living, breathing entity that changes with context, culture, and time. They taught us to be flexible in how we think about words and meanings.

Wittgenstein's language games teach us to appreciate the diverse ways in which language is used, while Derrida's deconstruction encourages us to look deeper, to find hidden meanings and question our assumptions. Together, these two philosophers offer a rich and dynamic perspective on how we communicate and understand the world around us.

As we continue our journey through "Words Unbound: The Labyrinth of Derrida and Wittgenstein", we'll discover more about how these ideas influence our perception of reality, our interactions, and our understanding of truth. So, let's keep exploring the fascinating architecture of language, guided by these two remarkable thinkers.

Chapter 3: The Edifice of Meaning

Welcome to the heart of our exploration – the world of meaning. In this chapter, we dive into how our two philosophers, Ludwig Wittgenstein and Jacques Derrida, approached the grand puzzle of meaning: how we create it, interpret it, and sometimes, get lost in it.

Building Blocks of Meaning: Wittgenstein's View

Imagine you're putting together a jigsaw puzzle. Each piece connects to the others in a specific way to create a complete picture. Wittgenstein saw the creation and interpretation of meaning in a similar way. He believed that the meaning of words is not something hidden inside them, waiting to be discovered. Instead, meaning is created through the way we use these words, like pieces of a puzzle coming together.

For Wittgenstein, the context – or the 'game' we are playing – is crucial. The word 'check' means something different in a restaurant than it does in a game of chess. He showed us that understanding a word's meaning involves understanding the activities and contexts in which it's used.

Unraveling Texts: Derrida's Approach

Now, let's shift to Derrida's perspective. If Wittgenstein's view of meaning is like assembling a puzzle, Derrida's approach is like examining a tapestry to see how it's woven. For Derrida, meaning in language is not fixed or stable. Instead, it's something that constantly shifts and changes, influenced by an endless play of differences.

Derrida suggested that when we read a text, we should look not just at what is said, but also at what is left unsaid – the spaces between the words, the assumptions, and the contradictions. He invites us to read between the lines, to see that every text contains the seeds of its own questioning.

The Limitations of Language

Both Wittgenstein and Derrida acknowledged that language has its limitations in capturing and expressing reality. Wittgenstein famously said, "Whereof one cannot speak, thereof one must be silent." This suggests that there are aspects of reality that language cannot touch, and we should recognize the boundaries of what can be expressed in words.

Derrida, on the other hand, showed us that language is inherently slippery and can never fully capture the essence of what we're trying to convey. He argued that the meanings we derive from texts are always open to interpretation and re-interpretation.

Parallel Paths in a Labyrinth of Words

Despite their different approaches, both philosophers guide us to a similar realization: language is a powerful tool, but it's not perfect. It shapes our understanding of the world, but it also has its blind spots and limitations. Understanding these limitations helps us appreciate the complexity and beauty of human communication.

As we navigate through the labyrinth of language and meaning, we realize that it's not just about arriving at a destination. It's about the journey – the playful, sometimes challenging, exploration of words and the meanings they carry. In the next chapters, we'll continue to explore how these ideas influence our perception of reality and our interactions with the world around us. Stay tuned as we delve deeper into "Words Unbound: The Labyrinth of Derrida and Wittgenstein."

Chapter 4: Beyond Words - The Realm of the Unsaid

In this chapter, we venture into a mysterious territory: the world of the unsaid, the unspoken, the silent. It's a realm that both Wittgenstein and Derrida explored, each in his own way. Here, we'll uncover the power of what is not said, and how it shapes our understanding of language and meaning.

Wittgenstein: The Unspoken Reality

Imagine watching a beautiful sunset. You're filled with awe, but when you try to describe it, words just don't seem enough. Wittgenstein was fascinated by this aspect of human experience – the things that we can show, feel, or know, but cannot fully express in words. He believed that some things, especially the most profound ones like beauty, ethics, or the mystical, lie beyond the reach of language. They are, in his view, "unsayable."

Wittgenstein suggested that these unsayable things are not meaningless. Instead, they show themselves in our actions, in art, in music, in the way we live. It's like knowing a person loves you not because they always say it, but because of how they act towards you. In Wittgenstein's world, what cannot be said can often be shown in other ways.

Derrida: The Echoes of Absence

Now, let's turn to Derrida. While Wittgenstein focused on the limits of what can be said, Derrida delved into what is absent in text – the unsaid that echoes between the lines. Think of reading a letter from a friend. The words tell you one story, but the pauses, the things they don't mention, tell you another. Derrida believed that understanding a text fully means paying attention to these gaps, to what is not written.

For Derrida, the unsaid is not just a lack or a void. It's a crucial part of how meaning is created. Every text, according to Derrida, is built on what it does not say, as much as on what it does say. This absence is not an emptiness but a space filled with potential meanings.

The Power of the Unspoken

Both Wittgenstein and Derrida teach us to respect the power of the unsaid. In a conversation, the pauses, the tone, the unspoken emotions can be as important as the words themselves. In a book, the implications, the suggestions, the unwritten thoughts can carry as much weight as the printed text.

Understanding this realm of the unsaid enhances our appreciation of language and communication. It encourages us to listen not just to the words spoken but also to the silences in between. It asks us to read not just for what is written, but also for what is implied, hinted, or left out.

In philosophical discourse, and indeed in everyday life, acknowledging the unsaid helps us grasp the complexity of communication and meaning. It reminds us that not everything can be captured in words and that sometimes, the most profound truths lie in the silent spaces of our interactions.

As we move through "Words Unbound: The Labyrinth of Derrida and Wittgenstein", we continue to explore these fascinating aspects of language and meaning, journeying deeper into the nuanced world of communication, where what is unsaid is as significant as what is said.

Chapter 5: Language, Power, and Society

In this chapter, we'll explore a fascinating aspect of language: its relationship with power and society. Both Wittgenstein and Derrida had profound insights into how language shapes, and is shaped by, the world around us. Let's delve into their thoughts and uncover the social and political implications hidden within our daily conversations.

Wittgenstein: Language as a Social Activity

Picture a group of people playing a board game. Each player understands the game's rules, and these rules determine how they play. Wittgenstein saw language in a similar light. He believed language is fundamentally a social activity, governed by rules we agree upon as a society. Just as the rules of a game shape how it's played, the norms of our language shape how we communicate and think.

Wittgenstein's perspective suggests that our understanding of the world is deeply influenced by the language we use. The words and structures of our language can limit or expand our thoughts. For example, the existence or absence of certain words in a language can affect how we perceive and categorize our experiences. This view implies that those who control language – such as media, educators, and leaders – can significantly influence how we see the world.

Derrida: Deconstructing the Power Dynamics of Language

Now, imagine a tapestry with intricate patterns. At first glance, it looks harmonious, but a closer look reveals conflicting threads and uneven stitches. Derrida approached language like examining this tapestry. He was interested in unpacking (or deconstructing) the hidden power dynamics within language.

Derrida argued that language is never neutral. It often reflects and perpetuates the power structures within society. For example, the way certain words are used can reinforce stereotypes or marginalize certain groups. By deconstructing language, Derrida aimed to reveal these hidden biases and challenge the status quo. His philosophy invites us to question the language we use and be aware of its implications.

The Social and Political Implications

Both Wittgenstein and Derrida show us that language is not just a tool for communication but a powerful force that shapes society. Wittgenstein's view encourages us to see how societal norms shape our language, and in turn, our thoughts. Derrida's approach urges us to look deeper and question the underlying power structures that language can subtly reinforce.

These philosophies have profound social and political implications. They remind us that the words we choose, the way we frame our sentences, and the narratives we construct can influence public opinion, shape cultural norms, and even affect policy making. Language can be a tool for empowerment or oppression, liberation or control.

In summary, this chapter highlights the significant role language plays in our social and political realms. As we journey through "Words Unbound: The Labyrinth of Derrida and Wittgenstein", we gain a deeper appreciation of the power of words and the responsibility that comes with using them. Understanding the connection between language, power, and society empowers us to use language more thoughtfully and effectively in our pursuit of a more just and understanding world.

Chapter 6: The Maze of Interpretation

Welcome to a chapter that's like a journey through a maze, a maze made of words, meanings, and interpretations. Here, we'll explore the challenges of understanding philosophical texts, focusing on the works of Derrida and Wittgenstein as our guides. We'll also discover the crucial role we, as readers, play in creating meaning.

Navigating Wittgenstein's Pathways

Imagine you're walking through a garden with many paths, each leading to different landscapes. This is akin to reading Wittgenstein's texts. His philosophy doesn't follow a straight line; instead, it takes you through various thoughts and observations about language, meaning, and understanding. Wittgenstein encourages us to see language as a tool with multiple uses, which means the meaning of words can change based on their context.

When interpreting Wittgenstein, the challenge is to embrace the journey and not just seek straightforward answers. His famous book, "Philosophical Investigations," is more like a collection of thought-provoking reflections than a traditional philosophical argument. As readers, we're invited to explore these reflections, ponder their meanings, and see how they apply to our experiences.

Unraveling Derrida's Textual Tapestry

Now, imagine you're unraveling a complex tapestry, finding different threads that intertwine, overlap, and sometimes contradict each other. This is what it feels like to delve into Derrida's deconstruction. Derrida believed that texts have multiple layers of meaning and that our understanding of them changes depending on our perspective.

Reading Derrida requires an open mind and a willingness to question our assumptions. His concept of deconstruction is not about destroying a text but about peeling back its layers to understand how it creates meaning. Derrida's famous work "Of Grammatology" is a prime example. It challenges readers to look beyond the surface and explore the deeper structures of language and meaning.

The Reader's Role in the Maze

In both Wittgenstein's and Derrida's works, the reader plays a vital role. We're not just passive receivers of information; we're active participants in creating meaning. As we read, our background, beliefs, and experiences influence how we interpret the text. This means that two people can read the same text and come away with different understandings.

This interactive process of reading highlights the dynamic nature of meaning. It's not fixed or static; it's something that evolves as we engage with the text. This also means that interpreting philosophical texts is not about finding the one 'right' meaning. It's about exploring the many possibilities, embracing ambiguity, and understanding that our interpretations are part of a larger conversation.

Embracing the Complexity

As we navigate the maze of interpretation, we learn to appreciate the complexity and richness of philosophical texts. Wittgenstein and Derrida, with their distinct approaches, teach us to be curious, reflective, and open-minded readers. They show us that the journey through the maze of meaning is not just about reaching an endpoint but about the insights we gain along the way.

So far, we've seen that interpreting philosophical texts is a challenging but rewarding adventure. It's an adventure that encourages us to think deeply, question our assumptions, and engage actively with the world of ideas.

Chapter 7: The Limits of Philosophy

In this chapter, we'll step into an intriguing territory: the boundaries of philosophical thought. Both Wittgenstein and Derrida, in their unique ways, shed light on what philosophy can and cannot do. Let's explore these limits and ponder the age-old question: Can philosophy provide definitive answers to its own problems?

Wittgenstein: Mapping the Boundaries

Picture philosophy as a map of a vast, unknown territory. Wittgenstein believed that this map has its edges, beyond which lies the unspeakable – things that we can experience but not express in words. He maintained that attempting to cross these lines and explore territories that language is unable to fully explain leads to a number of philosophical issues.

Wittgenstein famously said, "The limits of my language mean the limits of my world," implying that language alone can express what is possible for us to grasp. He believed that much of traditional philosophy tries to say the unsayable, leading to confusion and meaningless questions. In this view, the role of philosophy is not to answer all questions but to clarify what can and cannot be meaningfully discussed.

Derrida: Questioning the Foundations

Now, imagine a building with a complex, hidden foundation. Derrida invites us to inspect and question this foundation. He believed that philosophical inquiry often rests on assumptions and fixed ideas that need to be examined and challenged.

Derrida's approach, deconstruction, is not about demolishing the building of philosophy but about understanding its structure and the spaces within it. He showed that philosophical concepts are not as solid and unchanging as they might seem. By revealing the complexities and contradictions in these concepts, Derrida challenges us to rethink the foundations of our understanding.

The Debate: Can Philosophy Provide Definitive Answers?

This brings us to the central debate: Can philosophy solve the problems it sets out to address? Wittgenstein and Derrida, in their ways, suggest that philosophy's power lies more in questioning and clarifying than in providing final answers.

Wittgenstein's philosophy teaches us to recognize the limits of what can be discussed meaningfully. He guides us to find clarity in understanding these limits, suggesting that some of life's most significant aspects are beyond the reach of philosophical discourse.

Derrida, on the other hand, encourages us to continually question and deconstruct. His philosophy implies that there are always new layers to uncover, new perspectives to consider. In this view, philosophy is an ongoing process, a journey without a final destination.

As we journey through the landscapes of Wittgenstein's and Derrida's thoughts, we realize that the strength of philosophy might not lie in its answers but in its questions and the clarity it brings. Philosophy invites us to explore, to doubt, to understand, and sometimes, to simply acknowledge the mysteries beyond its scope.

Chapter 8: Legacy and Influence

In this chapter, we step back to appreciate the vast landscape influenced by the ideas of Jacques Derrida and Ludwig Wittgenstein. Their thoughts have rippled through not just philosophy but many other fields, enriching and challenging our understanding of language, culture, and society.

Echoes in Contemporary Philosophy

Imagine a conversation that started in a small room but eventually spread out into a vast auditorium. This is akin to how the ideas of Derrida and Wittgenstein have expanded into contemporary philosophical thought. Their concepts have become pivotal in discussions about language, meaning, and the nature of understanding.

Wittgenstein's idea of language games and the notion that the limits of our language are the limits of our world have influenced a broad spectrum of philosophical debates, from the nature of mind and consciousness to ethics and the philosophy of science.

Derrida's deconstruction has been a major force in postmodern philosophy. His emphasis on the instability of meaning and the importance of context and difference has inspired philosophers to re-examine how we construct knowledge and truth.

Beyond Philosophy: Literature, Psychology, and Politics

The impact of Wittgenstein and Derrida extends well beyond the bounds of traditional philosophy. In literature, Derrida's ideas have revolutionized literary theory, encouraging critics to look beyond the apparent meaning of texts and consider the play of language and the role of the reader in creating meaning.

In psychology, Wittgenstein's perspectives on language have influenced approaches to understanding how we think and communicate. His ideas have been particularly influential in areas like language acquisition and cognitive science.

In the realm of political science, both philosophers have made significant contributions. Wittgenstein's ideas about language and social practices have informed discussions on how societal norms and structures are created and maintained. Derrida's work has inspired critical examination of political discourse, emphasizing the power dynamics within language and how they affect societal structures and ideologies.

A Lasting Legacy

The legacies of Wittgenstein and Derrida are like rivers that have branched out into numerous streams, nourishing diverse fields and disciplines. They have challenged us to think about language not just as a means of communication but as a powerful tool that shapes our perception of reality.

In this book, we've explored the intricate paths carved out by these two thinkers. Their ideas continue to provoke and inspire, urging us to look deeper into the words we use and the worlds we create with them. As we close this chapter, we reflect on the profound impact these philosophers have had, not only on the field of philosophy but on the very way we understand ourselves and the world around us.

Chapter 9: Conclusion - Navigating the Labyrinth

As we reach the end of our journey , it's time to pause and reflect on the path we've traveled. This book has been an exploration into the intricate maze of language, meaning, and understanding, guided by the philosophies of Jacques Derrida and Ludwig Wittgenstein.

The Journey Through the Maze

We began by introducing Derrida and Wittgenstein, two philosophers who never met but whose ideas create a fascinating dialogue. We explored Wittgenstein's concept of language games, showing us that the meaning of words is shaped by their use in different contexts. We then delved into Derrida's deconstruction, an approach that encourages us to look beyond the surface of texts to uncover hidden meanings and contradictions.

We ventured into the edifice of meaning, examining how both philosophers deal with the creation and interpretation of meaning, and the limitations of language in capturing reality. We discovered the realm of the unsaid, exploring Wittgenstein's idea that some things can be shown but not said, and Derrida's focus on what is absent in texts.

Our journey took us through the connections between language, power, and society. We saw how Wittgenstein and Derrida's ideas reveal the role of language in shaping societal norms and power dynamics. We navigated the maze of interpretation, understanding the challenges of interpreting philosophical texts and the active role of the reader in creating meaning.

In exploring the limits of philosophy, we recognized that both philosophers highlight the boundaries of what can be meaningfully discussed and the importance of questioning and clarifying philosophical problems.

The Enduring Relevance of Derrida and Wittgenstein

As we conclude, it's clear that the philosophies of Derrida and Wittgenstein remain profoundly relevant in our modern world. Their insights into language and meaning are not just academic exercises; they have practical implications for how we communicate, understand each other, and interpret the world around us.

In an era of digital communication, social media, and global dialogue, their ideas help us navigate the complexities of language and meaning in new and evolving contexts. Wittgenstein's emphasis on the context-dependent nature of language and Derrida's focus on the layers of meaning and the role of the reader resonate strongly in a world where information is abundant, and interpretation is varied.

Embracing the Complexity of Language and Meaning

As we emerge from the labyrinth of Derrida and Wittgenstein's thoughts, we're equipped with a deeper appreciation for the complexity and beauty of language. We are reminded that language is a rich, dynamic process that forms our view of the world and ourselves, not just a means of expressing information.

"Words Unbound: The Labyrinth of Derrida and Wittgenstein" has been a journey of exploration, challenge, and discovery. As we continue to navigate the ever-changing landscapes of language and meaning, the ideas of these two philosophers light our way, reminding us to question, to listen, and to delve deeper into the words we use and the worlds they create.

About The Curious Philosopher

Welcome to The Curious Philosopher, your dedicated platform for diving deep into the world of philosophy. We are more than just a YouTube channel or a book publisher. We are a beacon of enlightenment, making complex philosophical concepts accessible and engaging for all.

Our YouTube channel is a rich repository of philosophy made simple. We take the profound and often complex ideas from the world of philosophy and break them down into digestible, easy-to-understand content. From the ancient wisdom of Socrates to the existentialist thoughts of Sartre, we cover a broad spectrum of philosophical schools and thoughts, making philosophy accessible to everyone, regardless of their background or prior knowledge.

As a book publisher, we take the same approach, transforming intricate philosophical theories into comprehensible narratives. Our books are not just collections of words, but vessels of wisdom that make philosophy approachable and relatable. We believe that philosophy should not be confined to academic circles, but should be available to all who seek to understand the world and their place in it.

At The Curious Philosopher, we believe in the power of curiosity and the pursuit of knowledge. We are here to stoke the fires of your curiosity, to guide you on your intellectual journey, and to help you navigate the fascinating world of philosophy.

If you are someone who is not afraid to question, to explore, and to learn, then you are in the right place. Join us on this journey of exploration, as we make philosophy easy to understand, one concept at a time.

Be sure to visit our Youtube channel at:
https://www.curiousphilosopher.com/youtube
You can also visit us on the web at
https://www.curiousphilosopher.com
Welcome to The Curious Philosopher. Stay curious. Stay enlightened.